A New True Book

DESERTS

By Elsa Posell

This "true book" was prepared
under the direction of
Illa Podendorf,
formerly with the Laboratory School,
University of Chicago

CHILDRENS PRESS, CHICAGO

18602

Saguaro cactus

PHOTO CREDITS

Lynn M. Stone—Cover, 2, 7, 12 (2 photos), 17, 18, 19 (left), 23 (2 photos), 26 (top right), 28, 44 (top)

Bill Thomas Photo—4

Harry Michalski—8, 14, 35, 42

Reinhard Brucker—9, 19 (right), 33 (right)

James M. Mejuto—10, 26 (top left, bottom), 32, 43

Louise T. Lunak—20, 31

Allan Roberts—22, 24, 25

James P. Rowan—33 (left), 34, 37, 44 (bottom)

Melaine Ristich—36, 38, 39, 40 (2 photos)

COVER—New Mexico—walking in the desert

Library of Congress Cataloging in Publication Data

Posell, Elsa Z.
  Deserts.

  (A New true book)
  Revised edition of: The true book of deserts. 1958.
  Summary: Describes the climatic conditions, flora, and fauna of the desert, and explains that some people find it habitable and others profitable for its mineral riches.
    1. Desert biology—Juvenile literature.
    2. Deserts—Juvenile literature. [1. Deserts]
  I. Title.
  QH88.P67   1982   508.315'4   81-15548
  ISBN 0-516-01613-X   AACR2

7 18 19 20 R 99 98 97

TABLE OF CONTENTS

Desert in Utah

DESERTS

Most deserts are hot and dry. Very little rain falls there. Sometimes it does not rain on the desert for a whole year.

When rain falls, it often comes hard and fast. Much of it does not sink into the ground. It runs off, instead.

Rain is often stopped by high mountains.

Winds blow in from the sea. They bring clouds. These clouds are heavy with water. The winds rise and cross the mountains. The clouds are cooled. Then rain falls. There is no rain left for the far side of the mountains. The dry land on the other side becomes a desert.

Hot, dry deserts have little rain.

Dune of the Sahara

The Sahara is in Africa.
It is the hot kind of desert.
Not all deserts are hot
places.

7

Tundra

Cold, frozen deserts have no heat.

There is a desert in Siberia called the tundra. It is the cold kind of desert.

The Painted Desert of Arizona

Deserts are not always
flat sand. Mountains and
rocks are found in some
deserts.

Wind-blown dune

Some parts of a desert might be hard clay. But hot, dry deserts have much sand.

Winds blow the sand into hills. These are called sand dunes. Sometimes the dunes are as high as tall buildings.

The desert bighorn (above) keeps cool in high mountains.
The cactus wren (below) lives in cactus plants.

DESERT ANIMALS

Many desert animals are different from animals found in other places. Desert animals can live in a hot, dry place.

Some desert animals sleep under rocks all day. Others burrow under the ground all day. They keep out of the hot sun.

Camel

Some deserts have sand-storms. Most desert animals can close their nostrils. This helps keep sand out of their noses. They can keep the sand out of their eyes and ears, too.

Desert animals have
tough skin over their lips.
They have strong teeth.
They can eat the spiny,
prickly plants of the desert.

A camel can live on the
desert. He does not have
to drink often. But when
he drinks, he drinks a lot.
He can drink about twenty
gallons of water at one
time.

Sometimes a camel does not eat for days. He then lives on the fat stored in his hump.

The camel has thick pads on his feet. These protect his feet from the hot sand. They also keep him from slipping.

A camel's eyes, ears, and nose keep out sand.

A camel has long
eyelashes. They protect his
eyes. Hair in his ears
keeps out the sand.

Collared
lizard

Many different lizards
live in the desert. Their
skins are scaly.

Many of them are the
color of the ground or of
plants. This helps protect
them from their enemies.
Enemies cannot see them
easily. Lizards also run
very fast.

A lizard tail can break off if an enemy grabs it. Some lizards can grow a new tail.

The chuckwalla lizard puffs up when it is frightened. No snake or bird can eat this lizard when it is puffed up.

Left: Chuckwalla lizard
Below: Desert skink

Horned toad

The horned toad is not a
toad. It is really a lizard.
Its head is covered with
spines like horns. These
are hard and rough. Few
animals try to eat this
lizard.

The horned toad is spotted brown and gray. It is hard to see.

The trade or pack rat is another animal found in the desert. This animal has large ears and big bright eyes. It gathers seeds and plants. Then it stores them for food. It also eats cactus plants.

Kangaroo rat

The kangaroo rat is also found in the desert. Its hind legs and tail are very long. Its front legs are short. It uses its front paws as hands and hops. like a kangaroo. It carries food in a pocket in each side of its mouth.

Desert turtle

The desert turtle has two
water sacs in its body. It
stores water in them. It
drinks only about once or
twice a year. Instead of
teeth, its jaws are like
small saws. It cuts food
with them.

Sidewinder rattlesnake

Many snakes live in the
desert. Some are harmless.
Some are dangerous. The
sidewinders and diamond-
backs are rattlesnakes.
They are poisonous.

The roadrunner is a bird of the desert. It is about two feet long from beak to tail. Its legs are long and strong. It is a fast runner. It can keep up with a car going twenty miles an hour.

Roadrunner

Top left: Saguaro cactus flowers
Top Right: Brittlebush and
senita cactus
Below: Hedgehog cactus flowers

26

DESERT PLANTS

In the spring the desert is pretty.

Bushes and wild flowers are in bloom.

The cactus plant is common on American deserts. Most cactus plants have no leaves. Some have tiny leaves for a short time only.

Arizona desert

The stems of cactus plants are thick. They help store water for the plants. These stems work as leaves do for trees and vegetables.

Roots of most cactus plants are near the top of the ground. The giant cactus has roots that spread far out. When rain falls, the roots can take in much water. Some of the water is stored in the stem.

Cactus stems are covered with a wax. This helps the plants keep in the water.

Many desert animals eat plants. The animals get their water from the plants.

The barrel cactus has only one stem. It is round like a barrel. Much water is stored in this stem. Animals make holes in this plant to get water or sap.

Barrel
cactus

The barrel cactus is
pretty. Its body is bright
green. Its thorns are pink,
red, and white. Its flowers
grow on top.

All cactus plants have prickles or thorns. These protect the plants.

Prickly pear cactus has prickles. Prickles are hard to remove when they get in our skin. This plant has a fruit like a pear. It is good to eat.

Prickly pear fruit

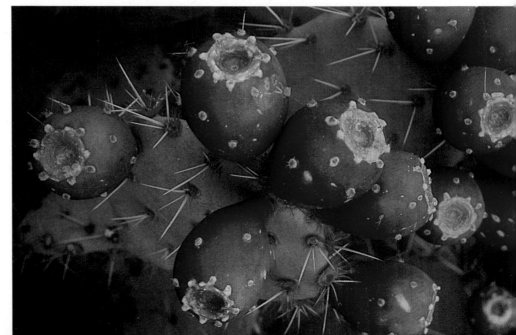

The leaves of the yucca (left) can be made into baskets (right).

Yucca plants have pretty flowers. Indians of the Southwest use their tough leaves. They make them into baskets.

Joshua tree

Joshua trees look strange. They are related to the yucca plant. They are tall. They have heavy trunks. The trunks have rough bark. The green-white Joshua tree flowers grow in bunches. The flowers have a nice smell.

The salt bush has leaves. They are white and soft. They taste salty. Sheep like the salt bush leaves.

Every desert has some spot that has water. It may be a spring. It may be a river. It may even be a well. This spot is called an oasis.

An oasis

Trees and shrubs grow around an oasis. They are green and colorful. Animals stop there and drink water. Desert travelers camp there. Sometimes people build homes at an oasis.

Monument Valley, Arizona

PEOPLE AND THE DESERT

Most people cannot live
in a desert. They cannot
grow food. They cannot
keep animals for meat and
milk.

Nomads herding animals across the desert

But some people do live in the desert. In some deserts are tribes of nomads. Nomads live in tents in the desert. They move from place to place. They search for the grass that grows after a desert rain.

Nomads wear heavy, loose clothes. These help keep out the heat of the sun. Nomads also know how to protect themselves in a sandstorm.

Nomads wear loose clothes.

Irrigation
canals

40

In many parts of the
world people have
changed the desert. They
have brought water to it.
Ditches and canals are
built. These bring water
from nearby rivers or from
mountain streams.

Desert well

Sometimes wells are dug.
They bring up water from
deep under the ground.

Bringing water to dry
land is called irrigation.
With irrigation, crops can
be grown. Cotton, grain,
fruit, and other crops can
be raised this way.

An oil well on the desert

Some deserts are rich
in minerals. Sometimes
people drill for oil in
deserts. Sometimes mines
are dug for other minerals.

Top: Prickly pear cactus and owl clover

Below: Teddy bear cholla cactus

About one-fourth of
Earth's land is desert.
Much of it is not used by
people. But as we learn
more about the desert, we
find that it can give us
food and other things. We
must be wise when we
use the desert.

WORDS YOU SHOULD KNOW

barrel(BARE • ul) — a round, large tub with a flat bottom and lid

burrow(BURR • oh) — to dig into the ground

cactus(KAK • tuss) — a desert plant with spines and no leaves

chuckwalla(CHUK • wall • uh) — a desert lizard that can puff itself up when afraid

dangerous(DAYN • jer • us) — able to cause harm

harmless — safe, not dangerous

hump — the raised part of a camel's back

irrigation(ear • uh • GAY • shun) — bringing water to dry land

Joshua tree(JOSH • oo • uh tree) — a tall desert tree

kangaroo rat(kang • uh • ROO rat) — a desert animal that looks like a kangaroo

lizard(LIZ • erd) — a kind of reptile that often lives on land

minerals(MIN • er • ruls) — something from the ground that people can use

nomad(NO • mad) — people who travel all the time

nostrils(NAHS • truls) — openings in the nose or snout

oasis(oh • AY • sis) — a spot where water is in the desert

poisonous(POY • zun • us) — full of something dangerous

protect(proh • TEKT) — keep safe

sac(SAK) — a part of the body like a pouch

Sahara(suh • HARE • uh) — a large desert in the north of Africa

scaly(SKAY • lee) — covered with tough, strong skin

sidewinder(SIDE • wine • der) — a snake that moves by going sideways

tough(TUFF) — strong and firm

tundra(TUN • druh) — a cold, frozen desert

yucca(YUK • uh) — a desert plant with tough leaves and pretty flowers

INDEX

About the Author

Elsa Posell received her M.S. in Library Science from Western Reserve University. She has been a librarian in the Cleveland Heights Public Schools, and is currently devoting over half her time to work with children in the Cleveland area and other Ohio counties in language arts, story telling, and creative writing. As a story teller and lecturer Mrs. Posell has worked in schools in Korea, Japan, Hong Kong, and China. One of her books, This is an Orchestra, *is published in Japanese. Mrs. Posell is also the author of* American Composers, Russian Music and Musicians, Russian Authors, *and* Beginning Book of Knowledge of Seashells.